D1010709

To those who weep
and
To those who weep with those who weep

CONTENTS

CONTENTS

FOREWORD

Ann Weems offers poetry and reflection more poignant than anything she has yet published. She brings to this task her finely contoured, well-seasoned faith, which is mature and knowing. She brings, as well, her peculiar finesse with words. She understands how speech operates and submits herself to the working of the words, which do things even beyond her will. When, however, Weems brings her faith and her speech to the task of utterance, she finds now that the task is saturated with pain and ache. The pivot point of her pain, perhaps the immediate trigger for her poetry, is quite concrete . . . an unfinished, unanswered, unresolved grief for her beloved Todd. Weems knows well that it takes all the faith she has and all the speech she has to honor the pain written deep in her life. And even then, it is scarcely enough for what is required.

The poems given here, however, are not preoccupied with the narrow range of self. Weems's gift as a poet is to move the listener in and through what is personal to her, so that the poem touches each of us in our concreteness and all of us in our commonness. For like the life of this poet, the life of the world is saturated with pain and ache not yet finished, not yet answered, not yet resolved. And we are left with the demanding question, What shall we do with so much of hurt that is left unfinished? Weem's powerful purpose is to speak it well.

In taking up the work of lament, Weems does not begin de novo. She is not the first in her craft to move pain unutterable to words uttered. Harold Bloom has taught us that every good poet rewrites the poems that are already there, using them in fresh ways, but never free from them. Weems knows quite self-consciously that her words have taken up residence in a large mansion of old griefs. And therefore to get said her concreteness, she must enter into that large mansion and respeak all the old griefs that are yet palpable in the world.

Weems's particular room in the world's mansion of uttered grief is the Bible, and more specifically, the Psalter. That book of poems-prayers-songs has funded the faith and imagination of synagogue and church since the birth of faith. What strikes one about the book of Psalms, if one notices anything at all, is that nearly one half of the Psalms are songs of lament and poems of complaint. Something is known to be deeply amiss in Israel's life with God. And Israel is not at all reluctant to voice what is troubling about its life.

It has been noticed by many readers of the Psalms before Weems that there is a recurring, disciplined form to the complaints and laments. Israel knew how to order its grief, not only to get that grief fully uttered and delivered but also to be sure that, said in its fullness untameable, it is not turned loose with destructiveness. What we have in these poems is not raw rage, anger, and sadness; rather what we have has already been ordered, mediated, and stylized to make the rage and hurt more effective, available, and usable. It is this ordering of raw grief that is the work of the poem and the gift of the poet.

The classic model of Israel's speech of grief, pain, and rage has six regular elements, which may occur in all sorts of configurations. Indeed, not all the elements need be employed in every such utterance.

1. The poem characteristically begins with the naming of God in an intimate address, for example, "My God, God of my fathers." The complaint is not uttered to a stranger. It is a trusting utterance set down in the middle of an ongoing friendship of trust and confidence. Neither is the lament spoken to "an empty sky." It is addressed to someone, aimed at a sovereign friend who is believed to be listening intently.

2. The poem moves immediately to complaint. It tells God, with some specificity, how troubled life is and what the trouble is. The complaint no doubt engages in hyperbole, much as a child does with a modest hurt. A child must overstate in order to secure the attention of a busy adult. The overstatement is perhaps intrinsic to pain. But it may also be a stratagem to get God's attention and to persuade God to act, for often the psalmist knows God to be absent, silent, indifferent, or uncaring. God must be "recruited" into the trouble.

3. The poem then comes to its focus in petition. This is the point of it all. The lament addresses God with a large, demanding, unapologetic imperative: "Turn, heed, save!" God can save, it is confessed, if only God can be mobilized. Everything to the speaker depends upon being able to mobilize God, for God's power is not in doubt. It is only God's attentiveness that seems in short supply, to which Israel's imperative makes strong appeal.

4. The complaint and petition under normal circumstances might be sufficient. But this is no normal circumstance. The urgent petitioner does not leave it at asking, but says more. The complaint is regressive speech. That is, the speaker in extremis does not credit God with noble, theological features. And therefore motivations are added to the petition, motivations that seek to give God some good reasons for acting. The motivations variously appeal to virtue, to repentance, to precedent, to God's honor, and even to God's vanity. The speaker often assumes that human needfulness is no adequate reason for which God may act. God must be shown that something is at stake for God in the trouble as well. Thus the motivations voice a dimension of faith that is not very respectable. But hurting people may on occasion risk the unrespectable, even the unorthodox.

5. Very often the needful speaker, who asks God for rescue from an enemy or an evildoer, does not stop at a petition for rescue. Very often the speaker would also like some vengeance against the enemy who has caused hurt. In addition to the good asked for self or for community, the lament also asks bad for the enemy. Thus there is frequently in these poems a wish for doing something hurtful and punishing and destructive to the human adversary. The pain risks what is most ignoble in human intention and daringly brings to speak what is darkest, and what is most unacceptable, in conventional theology and conventional social relations. These poems are, indeed, uttered in extremis.

6. Oddly enough, when the need, the hurt, the demand, and the venom are fully voiced, something unexpected happens in the psalm. The mood and tone of the psalm change. Israel's anger and protest appear to be spent, and pain characteristically moves to a positive resolution. The speaker is, at the end, confident of being heard and "dealt with bountifully," and so ends in rejoicing and praise. It is not at all clear what

happens that permits such a turn. But it is clear that such a turn belongs regularly to the pattern and genre of lament. It may be that the long protest is cathartic, and enough said finally suffices. Or it may be, as many scholarly readers think, that there was in the middle of the utterance a communal, liturgical intervention of assurance that permitted a new posture of confidence, well-being, and gratitude. On such a reading, the poem is genuinely dialogical. It receives an answer that resolves the need of the speaker. Thus the poem accomplishes something, and the speaker is, at the end of the poem, in a very different place.

It is true that the book of Psalms itself offers ample warrant for such a style of faith and speech. It is equally clear, however, that elsewhere in the Old Testament, named, known persons of faith engage in this sort of prayer, which transforms their life with God, their life in the world. Among these is Moses, Israel's great petitioner (Exod. 32:11–14, Num. 11:11–15), and Jeremiah (Jer. 12:1–6, 20:7–13), about whose life with God we seem to know the most. And beyond Moses and Jeremiah, the entire poem of Job is cast as a series of vigorous complaints in the mouth of Job, to which his friends make inadequate responses and to which God in the whirlwind makes an enigmatic and preemptive response. In all these examples that pervade Israel's text, we are able to see how Israel conducts itself when crowding into God's presence.

We may be fascinated by the artistic particularities of this genre of faithful utterance. But we should not miss the courageous and daring act of faith that is constituted and enacted in such utterance. The lament-complaint, perhaps Israel's most characteristic and vigorous mode of faith, introduces us to a "spirituality of protest." That is, Israel boldly recognizes that all is not right in the world. This is against our easy gentile way of *denial,* pretending in each other's presence and in the presence of God that "all is well," when it is not. But Israel also defiantly refuses to confess its guilt or to take responsibility for what is wrong in the world. Israel is able to identify "enemies" whose fault matters are, or Israel is able to hold God accountable for what is failed, dysfunctional, and unjust. Such speech is against our *docility* before God. Our Western propensity is to imagine God well beyond such strictures and such im-

plicatedness. Israel, however, thinks its way through trouble with real-
ism, and it speaks its truth without stammering.

In this strong act of faith, Israel rejects all the easy clichés conven-
tionally ascribed to God—omnipotent, omnipresent, omniscient, all-
loving, all-powerful—and seizes the initiative over against the Divine
Presence. Israel is not slowed down by our preference for "Prevenience"
or "Divine Sovereignty." Israel, in this speech, is more like a sweaty,
ominous General Haig, who is able to assert, "I am in charge here"—
and God must get accustomed to the new situation of conversation.
Israel holds the initiative and for the moment operates as God's senior
partner in faith, daring to dictate the terms of conversation for God. The
idea to which God must get accustomed is that Israel is not a docile kitty,
not easy putty in God's providential hands. Israel has will and voice and
starch. Israel knows its hurt to be unwarranted and unfair. And God must
make the best of Israel's new insistence.

To what end is such utterance? Well, perhaps in our psychologi-
cal propensity, the utterance is cathartic. One feels better afterward. Or
with more sophistication, there is need for an elegiac texture to a life not
as smoothly satiating as the TV ads have promised us. There is a wistful
artistry that heals through such utterance of self-disclosure. But no
"strong poet" will settle for the psychological or any thin artistry. This
utterance is a freighted theological act upon the Holy Powers of Heaven,
anticipating that such speech works new reality. This speech is indeed
"performative." And what it performs—requires—is a change in God's
life and God's dealings with the world. One cannot join this procession
of poets without imagining that grief said without apology demands that
God reenter the world in a different way, at a different place, in order
to do a different work. In place of "hands off," intervention. In place of
indifference, transformation. In place of sustenance, miracle. Such poets
may not invoke intervention or require transformation or produce mir-
acle. But what these poets confess—without a dissenting vote—is that
intervention, transformation, and miracle will not happen without such
utterance. In terms of bereftness, such utterances "from below" become
a sine qua non for notice from above. Newness starts "from below,"
where the poets live.

For that reason, the poet must utter on. Weems joins, one more time, that relentless, indispensable company. She does not need to imitate or to replicate old poets. But she is their child and their heir and their most recent echo. Her words will not fully resolve the hurt, as she well knows. Her utterance will not restore Todd, as she well knows. Her voice will not fully heal, as she well knows. Nonetheless, Weems in her verbal majesty becomes a sine qua non for our future. She joins the "strong poets," strong in faith, strong in utterance, strong in insistence, strong in risk. In having her and her words, we are represented, as Israel was represented, by such utterances. We are represented away from denial to strong, truth-telling protest. We are represented away from docility to daring intention. And in our being represented, God yet too must do differently. Our prayer to this newly positioned God is not louder than our thanks to beloved Ann. For by her wounded words, we may yet be healed.

WALTER BRUEGGEMANN
Columbia Theological Seminary

PREFACE

This book is not for everyone. It is for those who weep and for those who weep with those who weep. It is for those whose souls struggle with the dailiness of faithkeeping in the midst of life's assaults and obscenities. This book is for those who are living with scalding tears running down their cheeks.

On August 14, 1982, the stars fell from my sky. My son, my Todd, had been killed less than an hour after his twenty-first birthday. August 14, 1982 . . . and still I weep.

Many were there for me . . . family, friends, and people I didn't even know who sent their loving-kindness by mail or phone or in person. These tenderhearted ones were God-sent, and they have no idea how deeply they walked into my heart.

One of these people was Walter Brueggemann. He was enormously present to me and to my family. Concerned and caring, he kept in touch long after the sympathy notes stopped coming. One day he called and said I certainly didn't have to answer his question if I didn't want to, but he was working on Jeremiah and wanted to ask me, Will Rachel be comforted? I remember answering with little hesitation: No. No, Rachel will not be comforted. Not here, not now, not in the sense of being ultimately comforted. Of course, those people who are surrounding me with compassion are doing the work of angels, and I bid them come, but Rachel will be comforted only when God wipes the tears from her eyes.

It was then that Walter suggested I might want to write some lament psalms. I told him I might. Several months later, I sent him five lament psalms. I threw my copies in a desk drawer and slammed it shut.

Later that summer, Walter called me to ask if he could hand out

copies of my lament psalms to people attending a seminar he was lead-
ing. I told him the psalms were his; if people requested them, he could
give them copies, but I didn't know why they would want them. He
said, "Because throughout history the faithful have marched to the
throne of God and cried out in their pain. In your cries," he said, "you
are voicing the sobs of these people."

Shortly thereafter I began receiving letters and phone calls from
people who had been in Walter's seminars. Their stories, like mine, were
painful, too painful for any of us to try fitting our souls into ten correct
steps of grieving. They knew what I knew: There is no salvation in self-
help books; the help we need is far beyond self. Our only hope is to
march ourselves to the throne of God and in loud lament cry out the
pain that lives in our souls.

I went for long periods of time when I did not write a lament
psalm. Then I would find myself before God with tears streaming down
my face, and another psalm would be thrown into that drawer. Only
when I finished them last summer was I able to put the manuscript in
the drawer without slamming it shut.

Of course, I know my psalms are not finished. Anger and alleluias
careen around within me, sometimes colliding. Lamenting and laughter
sit side by side in a heart that yearns for the peace that passes under-
standing. Those who believe in the midst of their weeping will know
where I stand.

In the quiet times this image comes to me: Jesus weeping.

> Jesus wept,
>> and in his weeping,
>>> he joined himself forever
>>> to those who mourn.
>> He stands now throughout all time,
>>> this Jesus weeping,
>>>> with his arms about the weeping ones:
>> "Blessed are those who mourn,
>>> for they shall be comforted."
>> He stands with the mourners,
>>> for his name is God-with-us.
> Jesus wept.

"Blessed are those who weep, for they shall be comforted." Some-
day. Someday God will wipe the tears from Rachel's eyes.

> In the godforsaken, obscene quicksand of life,
> there is a deafening alleluia
> rising from the souls
> of those who weep,
> and of those who weep with those who weep.
> If you watch, you will see
> the hand of God
> putting the stars back in their skies
> one by one.

ANN WEEMS

Psalms of Lament

Lament Psalm One

O God, have you forgotten my name?
How long will you leave me
in this pit?
I sang hosannas
all the days of my life
and waved palm branches
greened in the new spring world.
Rich only in promises
from you,
I followed
believing,
and then they killed him
whom I loved
more than my own life
(even that you taught me).
They killed him
whom you gave to me.
They killed him
without a thought
for justice or mercy,
and I sit now in darkness
hosannas stuck in my throat . . .

Why should I wave palm branches
or look for Easter mornings?
O God, why did you name me Rachel?
A cry goes up out of Ramah,
and it is *my* cry!
Rachel will not be comforted!

Don't you hear me,
you whose name is Emmanuel?
Won't you come to me?
How long must I wait
on this bed of pain
without a candle
to ward off the night?

Come, Holy One,
feed to me a taste of your shalom.
Come, lift to my lips
a cup of cold water
that I might find my voice
to praise you
here in the pit.
Pull forth the hosannas
from my parched lips,
and I will sing to all
of your everlasting goodness,
for then the world will know that
my God is a God of promise
who comes to me
in my darkness.

Lament Psalm Two

God, find me here
where the sun
is afraid to shine!
Don't you recognize
your faithful one?
Haven't I known you
since the days of my youth?
Haven't I sung your songs
in the ears of your enemies?
Why then are you silent?
Why have you forsaken me
and left me to wail
in the empty night?
Why do you give me silence
when I ask for
the nightingale's song?

O God, have pity on me
and enter into
the city of my pain.
Hear my cry
and come to me
that all might know
your faithfulness.
From the icy coldness
of the pit,
I will praise your name,
for like a shepherd
searching for a lost sheep,
you will not give up
until you find me.

Here in the gloom
I wait for the light
of your coming.
Then I will shout
that my God is the God
who does not rest
until all are
gathered in
from the threat of night.

Lament Psalm Three

How large a cup of tears must I drink, O God?
How much is enough?
Must my cup grow and overflow
even as I drink from it
until it becomes
as deep as a well
and I can't swallow anymore?

God, do you forget
your servant?
Do you mistake me
for some other
who did not
serve you,
love you,
yearn for you,
that you could snatch
from me
this precious treasure,
this child
who spent his life
loving you?
What kind of cruel judgment is this?
Don't you want the unbelievers
to see
that you bless your own?
Will I weep
all the days of my life?
Will you forget me
forever?

Remember me, God,
remember your promise to me
to wipe away my tears . . .
Come into my pain
that I may once more
praise your name
in the streets of the city.

Give me hope, O God;
come in your steadfast love
to meet me.
Then will I sing loud
psalms of praise
to my God
who does not forget me.
I will sing
loud psalms of praise
in the morning light,
and all who hear
will join in
with joyful voices,
for our God does not forget us.

Lament Psalm Four

O Holy One, I can no longer see.
Blinded by tears
that will not cease,
I can only cry out to you
and listen
for your footsteps.

Are you, too, O God,
blinded by tears?
Have you watched this world
pile its hate
onto the faces
of your little ones
until your eyes are so filled with tears
that you cannot see me
waiting for you?
Are you, O God,
deafened by the expletives
of destruction and death?
Have you heard
so many obscenities
that you cannot hear
my moaning?
O God, if you are blind,
can't you hold out
your hand to me?
If you're deaf,
can't you call my name?

How long, O God,
am I to sit
on the plain of blindness?

How long am I to listen
to the profanity
of my enemies
who mock:
"Where is your God now?"

Show them, O my God,
that you remember.
Reach out your hand
and dry my eyes
that I might see
a new beginning.
Open your mouth
and call me by name
that I might know
you remember me.
Claim me that I might
announce in the marketplace
that my God is here.

O my heart,
give thanks!
My God is here even
in the midst of destruction.

Lament Psalm Five

O God, find me!
I am lost
in the valley of grief,
and I cannot see my way out.

My friends leave baskets of balm
at my feet,
but I cannot bend to touch
the healing
to my heart.
They call me to leave
this valley,
but I cannot follow
the faint sound
of their voices.
They sing their songs
of love,
but the words fade
and vanish in the wind.
They knock,
but I cannot find the door.
They shout to me,
but I cannot find the voice
to answer.

O God, find me!
Come into this valley
and find me!
Bring me out of this land
of weeping.

O you to whom I belong,
find me!
I will wait here,
for you have never failed
to come to me.
I will wait here,
for you have always been faithful.
I will wait here,
for you are my God,
and you have promised
that you counted the hairs on my head.

Lament Psalm Six

O God, why do you leave me
face down in my memories?
Eyes wide open . . .
every nerve exposed . . . ?
Why do you leave me all alone
in the house of memories?

Open the door, O God!
Burst in and seize me
from the hell
of remembering!
Remembering the smile
the voice
the whistle
the love.

Take me from here, O God!
Please be merciful!
Blot out the memories!
Pick me up from the mire of pain!
Lead me away to the place of peace,
for you are my God,
and you will not
you will not
abandon me!

Lament Psalm Seven

O God, you've allowed death to take him away,
leaving me alone
in the chill dawn of unfinished love.
What could you have been thinking?

Ungiven gifts pile about me.
Unsung songs remain
trapped in my throat.
Unsaid words lie rotting
in my mouth,
and I sit staring down
a lifetime of unlived days,
for love didn't leave
when death arrived.

God, what will I do
with the unfinished love?
It wells up within me
with nowhere to go,
and I am bursting
with the pain of it.

Come to me, O Comforter,
come to me.
Hold me against the pain
for just awhile
so that I might catch my breath.
Come to me, O Comforter,
and give me peace.

O God, I don't understand all this.
Give me your peace
that passes understanding.
Give me the grace
that only you can give,
the grace that overflows with peace,
so that I might spend my days
telling all who would hear
that you, O God—
you are the answer.

Lament Psalm Eight

God, have you forgotten our covenant?
Have you forgotten your promise?
Can't you enter my world of tears?
Can't you make your home
in a heart that is broken?
O God, acknowledge that
you hear my cry!
Send word that you
are on the way!
Answer me so that
I can cling to some hope
of your presence,
for I have believed
that you would come.
I have trusted that
you would keep your word.

I will praise your name
through my tears
and continue to worship you,
my hope and my life,
for you are merciful and just,
and compassion is your name.
You will be with me;
you will bless and keep me,
and I will live in
your abundant love
for all time.

Lament Psalm Nine

Come to me, O God;
set me free from this agony.
O God, O God, O God,
please help me!

Every waking moment is filled
with the pain of that moment.
Every night is filled with
terror and with fear.
O God, how did it happen?
Where were you?
Why didn't you stop it?
O God!
All's wrong with the world!

It is my voice, O God,
that sobs to you
before the day breaks.
Like a balloon that is released
to the sky,
my prayer makes its way
to you, O God,
before the sun rises.
Everywhere I turn,
doors are slammed shut.
O God,
do not slam the door
of heaven
in my face!

O God,
the world has been drained
of color!
The music has been turned off!
The silent shroud
covers any green that remains.
All is grey
and smells of death.
I fear for the death
of my spirit,
O God.
I wrestle
to hold onto
the deep places
of my inner being.
My soul is in danger.
Save me,
O God,
save me!

Consider my weeping,
O Holy One,
be tenderhearted
when you speak
to me.
Handle my bruised heart
with gentleness,
for without you,
I am nothing.

O God, you speak,
and the sky is alive
with music!

Your hand reaches out
and colors the world
with a touch!
My soul is a rainbow!
My sobbing bursts
into song!
My God is here!

Lament Psalm Ten

O God, I can't stand it!
I pace like a caged animal;
I cry to the point of exhaustion;
my head aches unceasingly;
my heart feels as though it will
fall from my chest.
Over and over I scream your name,
but you do not answer . . .
and you do not come . . .
and I cannot stand it.

O God, I know your ways
are not our ways,
so I do not ask
for a mighty army
to rescue me.
I do ask
that you send lambs
to save me
and birds to guard my door.
I do ask
for your blessing
so that I might stand again
against your enemies,
and take my place once more
in the company of your people.

O God, I celebrate our covenant!
Nothing can separate me
from your love!

Lament Psalm Eleven

Don't I belong to you anymore, O God?
Don't you claim me as one of your people?
Have you had a change of heart?
Have you turned against me?
Did I do something unforgivable?

O God, remember to remember.
When you see the bow of the rain in the sky,
remember that you are my God.
Remember and come to me.
Remember your promise
to be my God.
Be merciful to me.
O Holy One, call me by name.
Walk with me
in the valley of shadows.
Do not leave me,
for you are my God
and I belong to you.

You are everything,
the beginning and the end
and life in between.
All praise to you, my God, my life, my heart, my soul!

Lament Psalm Twelve

O God, what am I going to do?
He's gone—and I'm left
with an empty pit in my life.
I can't think.
I can't work.
I can't eat.
I can't talk.
I can't see anyone.
I can't leave my house.
Nothing makes any sense.
Nothing seems worth doing.

How could you have allowed this to happen?
I thought you protected your own!
You are the power:
Why didn't you use it?
You are the glory,
but there was no glory in his death.
You are justice and mercy,
yet there was no justice, no mercy for him.
In his death there is no justice for me.

O God, what am I going to do?
I'm begging you to help me.
At least you could be merciful.
O God, I don't remember a time
when you were not my God.
Turn back to me;
you promised.
Be merciful to me;
you promised.

Heal me;
you promised.
My heart is broken.
My mind is broken.
My body is broken.
Nothing works anymore.
Unless you help me
nothing will ever work again.

O Holy One, I am confident
that you will save me.
You are the one
who heals the brokenhearted
and binds their wounds.
You are the power
and the glory;
you are justice
and mercy.
You are my God forever.

Lament Psalm Thirteen

O God, even my friends
bring me books
with ten steps
to overcome grief
as though healing
comes in paperback,
and filling my time
with one-two-threes
will bring peace
to my soul
and energy to my body.

Why don't they try
to understand?
The worst of all
are those who say
I must accept his death
as though his death
is acceptable.
No!
His death is unacceptable!
And I will not be comforted!

In my suffering
I am told I must
grieve correctly.
O merciful God!
What are they doing?
Aren't we supposed
to go to you
with our tears?

Isn't it in your word
that we will be
comforted?

I come to you, Holy One,
for I know
my salvation
is not in "coping,"
but is in hope,
hope that comes
only from you.

O God, in your time
the scales will fall
from my heart
and I will see again,
and seeing, I will fall
to my knees
in thanksgiving
to you, O Gracious One,
only to you.

Lament Psalm Fourteen

What have I done to deserve this?
What terrible sin have I committed
that you would leave me in this pit
with no light
with no warmth
with no hope?
Why, O God, are you treating me
as though you do not know me?
What is it I've done?
Have you looked into my heart
and found me so wanting?
I've never claimed to be good, O God,
for none but you are good,
but I have tried
to follow your ways.
I have tried
to be faithful.
Over and over I've failed,
but I've tried
to understand your word.
I've asked for forgiveness
and tried again . . . but now
your silence is destroying me,
and your enemies call me fool.
I have believed, O God;
I do believe.
I do believe
you will hear me
and bring me out
of the mouth of death.

I do believe
that in your holiness
your grace will save me,
and I will live
in you once more,
for you, O Holy One,
will not desert me!
Just the sound of your name
on my lips
brings hope.

Lament Psalm Fifteen

O God, why have you abandoned me?
I sit and wait for you and
you do not come.
I watch everyone who passes,
but it is not you.
I sit by myself
on the side of life
and cry to you,
but you do not come.
I stand and look
from the window,
but you are nowhere
in sight.
I need you, O God,
but you have left me
all alone.
I try to talk myself
into believing
that you're on the way,
perhaps tomorrow,
or the next day . . .
but you do not appear.
How can I walk in this pain
all alone?
How can I stand knee-deep
in suffering without you?
Where are you,
O God of my life?
Where are you
when I'm in such danger?

Will you let me slip away simply
because you didn't get here on time?
O God of mercy, do not
abandon me.
Show your face
at my window
and wipe the tears
from my life.
Please come to me.
Please
take care of me.

I will shout your name
from the rooftops!
I will dance your praise
among the stars.
I will tell the world
that you would never
abandon me.

Lament Psalm Sixteen

O God, will this night never end?
Give me sleep, O God!
Give me rest!
Erase from my memory
the moments of his death.
Blot out the terror
and the ever-present fear
and let me sleep.
I lie upon this bed
tortured by thoughts
that come unbidden.
The night is full of demons.
They stand upon my heart
until I cannot breathe.
There is nothing in my world
this night except his death.
O God, bring the morning light.

Is it not enough
that he is dead?
That there is nothing
I can do
to change what is?
Must I spend each night
revisiting the unlit
corridors of death?

O God, be merciful!
Bring the dawn!
Come into this night
and tear it into day!

O my God, you are hope.
You take the bonds of death
and break them
into pieces of life.
The demons of the night
cower and hide
from the brilliance
of your presence.
You alone can banish the night
and create the sweet stream
of morning's light.
There is none who can stop you,
for you are the God of light
and the light of my soul.

Lament Psalm Seventeen

O God, I live in the land of the forgotten.
I stretch out my hand to you,
and there is nothing.
I cry night and day,
and you do not take pity on me.
I pray to you,
but you turn away.
O God, why won't you help me?

You show compassion to your enemies
and long for the faithless to return to you.
Yet I have worshiped you
since I was a child,
and have lived in covenant with you.
Yet, like a fly,
I am brushed away
from your throne
as though I didn't belong
in your presence.
How long will I have to live
outside your holiness?
How long will I have to endure
the unholy hell
of the presence of death?
How long will I have to feel
the ever-fresh wound
of the absence
of him whom I loved?
Undo it, O God!
Give him back!

O God, why did you create a life
that includes death?
Why did you create us
to love one another
and then take from us
the ones we love?
O God, take me from the land
of the forgotten;
let me rest once more in you.
Push death out of my face
and hold me in the palm of your hand.

I know in my heart that
you will not forget me.
Your grace is all-encompassing,
and your love has no conditions.
You, O God, will not forget me,
for you have made covenant with me,
and your covenant is forever and ever.

Lament Psalm Eighteen

O God, why have you left me in the wilderness
with no bread?
I hunger for your righteousness;
I am starved for your justice.
O God, feed me!
My soul is starving
without your nourishment.
I need you;
why have you left me
in this desolate land?
Are you ashamed to be my God?
Will you no longer welcome me
into the city you are building
for the faithful?
Is there no end to my loss?
Must I lose my heart
and now my soul?

Listen to me, O God:
My soul is shriveling within me.
It is hard and crusty
and needs to be watered
with your holy spirit.
My soul is numb
with neglect.
Why are you ignoring me?
O God who counts
the birds of the air,
have mercy on my soul.

Take away the bitter herbs
and bring me the bread of life
so that I might have the strength
to join those who gather together
to praise your holy name.

My soul cries out to you;
my soul longs for you.
Remember me, Holy One,
for you are my Alpha and Omega.

Lament Psalm Nineteen

What do they celebrate in the sanctuary, O God?
And of what do they sing in joyful procession?
In their exuberance their voices
fill the sky with song,
and my ears are filled
with their praise of you,
their songs of thanksgiving
for your advent.
How can I join their singing, O God,
if you do not come to me?
How can I shout "gloria"
if you will not advent here?

O my God, there is an inn in my heart
where the door is open to you;
please, Holy One,
be born anew to me.
Please come into my misery.
Please live in my despair.
Do your birthing in my manger
so that I may once again
hear in my heart
the good news of great joy.
Send an angel, O God,
to announce that
you have heard my cry
and will come to me in my sorrow.
Then, O God, I will once again
be able to tell the story
of this thing that has happened
in my heart.

Once again my voice will be raised
and I will sing in procession
and celebrate in the sanctuary
and with the angels praise
your holy name.

Glory to you, O God,
who advents even into the life
of one who weeps the day away.
Glory to you in the highest,
for you are not ashamed
to walk with me in darkness.
You have heard my cry
and turned to me,
and I have seen a great light.

Lament Psalm Twenty

Save me, O God, from your enemy!
I have met evil face to face.
Its terrible eyes bored into my soul;
it strangled my heart with icy fingers,
and I was thrown to the ground.
I cried out to you, O God,
and you left me on the plain of souls
to wrestle for life.
Weakened and wounded,
my being overflows
with the hot burning tears of the lost.
The Evil One pushes me to the brink;
his eyes gleam with delight
to see how helpless I am.
He laughs loudly at my tears
and my cries to you.

O you whose face I long to see,
how long, O Lord, how long
before you come
to rescue me
from the grip of the Evil One?
Claim me, O God;
pull me from his grasp
and set me free to live again.
Unleash in me a newness
that will stun the Evil One.
Pull my soul from his deathly teeth
and stupefy him with your power.

O God, your ways are wondrous.
Your voice commands the universe.
You answer my cry and evil flees.
You answer my prayer
and my soul breathes.
Thank you, O God;
you are the very breath of my being!

Lament Psalm Twenty-one

O God, will it never stop?
Pain falls on pain
like snow on snow.
Just when I think I might stand,
I am pushed down again.
Is there no end to it?

The wound cannot close,
for it's constantly hit.
The infection oozes pus,
and I am beginning to think
that I will be fevered forever.
Is there no hope
that I can wake to laughter?
Is there no end to the tears?

Only you, O Holy One,
can stop the avalanche.
Only you can dig beneath
the pus to find me.
Only you can wipe my brow
and close the wound.
Come, O Healer, come
and give me hope,
for I have trusted in you
as those who came before me.
We trusted
and called upon your name
and you held out your hand
and closed our wounds
and pulled us to our feet.

I know, O Healer of Souls,
that you are not far away.
I know, O Physician of the Heart,
that you will not forsake me,
but will stitch my wounds
and gently restore my soul.
I will gain the strength
to serve you once more,
for you are my health
and my joy.

Lament Psalm Twenty-two

I don't know where to look for you, O God!
I've called and I've called.
I've looked and I've looked.
I go back to my room
and sit in the dark
waiting for you.
Could you give me a sign
that you've heard?
Could you numb my emotions
so I wouldn't hurt so much?

I walk in circles.
I rock in my chair.
I pour a glass of water.
I look out the window.
I walk to the kitchen.
I open the refrigerator;
there's nothing I want.
I close it again.
I turn on the TV.
The voices are too loud;
the faces are too loud.
I mute the voices;
I turn off the faces.
The silence is my friend;
the silence is my enemy.
I go upstairs.
I lie on the bed.
I get up again.
I walk to the window.

No sign of you!
I'm dying, O God, without you.

O God of wonder,
you can change it all.
You can distract me
from thoughts of death.
You can fill my days with purpose.
You can make the nights shorter.
You can let me find you.
Don't hide from me any longer, O God.

O God,
you reveal yourself to those
who call upon your name.
Blessed be my God
who does not fail me!

Lament Psalm Twenty-three

Speak to me, O my God,
speak to me!
Tell me you will help me;
tell me in a loud voice!
Let me hear words of mercy
from your mouth,
words that will flood my heart
and make it beat again.

O God, in times past,
you have heard the groaning
of your people,
and you have spoken to them;
you have saved them.
Speak to me now, O Holy One,
to me, O God,
the one who waits for your word.
Speak to me so that I can
return to life,
and follow you once more.
Speak, O my God,
speak to me,
the language of your heart.
Speak and I will run
among your people.
All who have the ears to hear
will marvel that your word
has made my feet dance.
To you, O God, goes the glory
always,
for in your word
I find my life.

Lament Psalm Twenty-four

O my God, it is not fair!
I watch other people
come and go.
They walk and talk
and eat and play.
They laugh; they travel; they work;
they marry and give birth,
but we sit around the table of death.
We do not smile, nor do we live.
We are suspended in that one moment,
that one moment of death.
When his life was taken,
our lives were forever changed.
O our God, why aren't you fair to us?
Why were we the ones chosen
to weep?

It is not fair, O God!
Everybody knows we belong to you.
We declared it in the sanctuary.
Why, O God of mercy,
do we sit at the table of death?
Move us, O God of power; move us
to the table of life!
Give us bread and give us wine
in the name of your son
let us live again!

If you would just
break the bread of life
over our heads,
the crumbs would be sufficient.
If you would just pour the wine
close to us,
the splash would revive us.

O God of glory,
our dead hearts beat again.
The hosannas rush out of our mouths,
and we bow down
in the presence of our God
who is life eternal.

Lament Psalm Twenty-five

O God, what has happened to your creation?
What kind of world is this
that the innocent die?
Where is your hand
that it does not stop the killing?
How long will you watch
while the world calls you names?
How long will you wait
while the river of blood
floods your streets?
Will you let the innocent die
and the guilty go free?
Will the guilty laugh cruelly
in the streets,
while the innocent lie cold
in their graves?

O God, where is your holiness
in the face of this hell?
Bind the guilty, O God,
and free the innocent
to live in your presence.
Open their graves,
and take them to your heart.
Kiss their cold lips
and let them live forever
in your eternal shalom.

O Holy God, I am stunned
that you sit by
while the innocent cry to you.

Where is your righteous anger?
Where is your powerful hand?
Why are your enemies allowed
to desecrate your creation
and slaughter your children?

O God of mercy, I am on my knees!
I beg you to bring peace
out of this chaos.
Divide the Red Sea once more
and save your people.
Come from your heaven
and scoop the little ones
into your arms
and hold them
against the terrors of this world.

O God of justice, stop these plagues,
and stoop to comfort your people,
for you, and you only, are our refuge.

Lament Psalm Twenty-six

I am on my knees, O God,
asking for your help,
but you do not give it.
I constantly seek you,
but I do not find you.
I stand at your door and knock
but it is not opened to me.
I'm asking for a fish;
don't give me a snake.
I'm asking for an egg;
don't give me a scorpion.
I'm hungry
for your presence,
O God.
I'm starving
for your holiness!
Even we sinners know
how to give good gifts
to our children.
Give me then, O my God,
your holy spirit.

O God, I will continue
to ask, to seek, to knock,
for you are the door of hope,
and you will let me in,
and you will say to me:
"I am your God,"
and I will bow down,
and I will receive,
and I will find.

And the door will be
opened to me,
and I will live
in your blessing,
and my mouth
will be forever
full of praise
for my God.

Lament Psalm Twenty-seven

O God of my heart,
it is your name I call
when the stars do not come out.
O God of my soul,
it is to you I turn
when the torrents of terror
drown me.
O God of mercy,
it is for your hand I reach
when I stumble
on the stones of sorrow.
O God of justice,
it is to you I cry
when the landslide of grief
buries me.

I stand beneath the night
where stars used to shine
and remember
gazing mesmerized
at the luminaries of the sky
until I could walk
the ink-blue beach
between their shining.
Then their shining stopped,
for they left the sky,
and you, O God,
left with them.

And I am left
alone
beneath a starless sky
with a starless heart
that barely beats.

Will your stars
never shine again?
Will they never again
speak of your mystery?
Will they never again sing
their songs
to my soul?
Will I never again know
the wonder
of the God
of star and sky?

O God of my heart,
peel back the night
and let the starlight
pour out upon
my upturned face.
Let my eyes drink
a sky of stars.
Let my heart bathe
in the stunning light
until my soul sings again
with the conviction
of the faithful.

In your mercy and justice,
O God of my heart,
call me by name,
and the stars will shine
once more,
as they did
on that morning
when they first began
to sing.

Lament Psalm Twenty-eight

O God, hear me!
I am tormented
by the finality of death
and harassed by those
who want to explain it . . .
As though the pain
of his death
is not enough,
their glibness cuts
like a razor
into my heart
and the bleeding starts
again.
O God, have pity on me
and keep them from my doorstep!

Why, O God, do I have to
deal with them?
They crouch by my door;
their whispered voices
fly in through my window:
"He was in the wrong place
at the wrong time."
O God of my life!
Tell me you were there, too!
Tell me that on your earth
there is no wrong place
nor is there any wrong time
for the children of God!
Tell me you caught him
in your arms
and wiped the tears

from his eyes,
and showed him your face
as you had showed him
your heart.
Tell me you are always
with us
in life and in death.

Have pity on me, O God,
and keep them from my doorstep!

O God, they're like magpies,
suggesting his death is a test
of my faith,
as though you are some
egomaniac God
who zaps me from on high,
who demands repeated assurances
of my love,
as though you do not know
my heart!

Have pity on me, O God,
and keep them from my doorstep!

O God, I know you
are not what they say!
That you loved him
so much
that you wanted him
to live
in heaven with you!
O God, they blaspheme you
and trivialize his death!

Have pity on me, O God!
And keep them from my doorstep!

In my suffering, O God,
my ears are inflamed
by their mouths
like megaphones
telling me
it is your will.
I know you,
O God of love,
I know you,
and your will is life;
your name is compassion.
O God of mercy,
send them away!
Let them leave me
to my weeping.
Let them leave me
with the quiet ones
who sit beside me
through the days.
Let them leave me
with your word
open upon my heart.
Send them away,
but write once more
upon their hearts
and upon mine
the word of your love.

O merciful God,
there is no trouble
I cannot bring to you!
In you only is my trust!

Lament Psalm Twenty-nine

Night after night
I collect my tears
and send them to you, O God.
Night after night
I come before you,
tear-stained.
Have mercy on me.
Hear my weeping
and turn your heart to me.

I weep for what was
and will never be again.
I weep for a future
that is no longer possible.
I weep because I love.
Like a willow
on the bank of a river,
I'm bent
from the weight of my tears.
They flood my world,
and there is no stopping
their force.
Save me, O God, from drowning!
O God,
have you covered your ears
to my weeping?
Have you covered your eyes
so you won't see me
going under?
Have you forgotten me
night after night?

Didn't you hear your son
weeping over Jerusalem?
Didn't you count his tears
when Lazarus died?
Didn't you see
how deeply moved he was
when Mary wept?
O God, acknowledge me,
for night after night
I collect my tears
and send them to you.

I trust in you, O God,
for your hand
can divide the waters,
or gently wipe the tears
of the grieving ones.
I trust in you, O God,
day after day.

Lament Psalm Thirty

The pain continues to wave over me!
Stop it, O God,
please stop it!

I live in unceasing disarray.
Chaos grasps my ankles,
turmoil keeps me
stirred and stressed,
and I am all alone.
No one knows;
no one really knows!

I think I'm in control,
but I can't stop
the undulating ache
that wells up suddenly
and overwhelms me
until I collapse
from grief.
My emotions hold
my body captive,
and my soul slides
on shaky ground.
I cannot speak.
Who, O God,
will speak for me?
I cannot stand.
Who will hold me up
on my journey?
Who, O Holy One,
if not you?

Surely you will not
turn against me
when I cry for help!

My whole life is yours, O God.
If I have to crawl,
I will struggle
to stay on your path.
Don't let me faint
and lose my place!
Don't let me fall away!

Stop this deluge of misery!
Speak for me, O God!
In the midst of the people,
speak for me!
Hold on to me as I walk,
so I won't get separated
from those
along the holy way.
I am bruised,
but you will heal me,
for I know you,
O God of history.
You are the way
and the truth
and the life.
You are *my* way
and *my* truth
and *my* life.

I am a dimly burning wick,
but you will not quench me.

I will speak again
and walk again
and you will take
my pain,
and the warmth
of your hand
will dissolve it,
and I will clap for you
forever.

Lament Psalm Thirty-one

How long will you watch, O God,
as your people live huddled in death?
The whole world
is dressed in tears,
and I have joined
the procession of the bereaved
who walk daily in the death places.
We drown in the sea.
We bleed on the battlefield.
We lie stricken on sickbeds.
We are judged in the courtrooms.
We are victims of crime.
We are homeless and hungry.
Is this not enough?

We are tormented by mental illness.
We are abandoned by loved ones.
We wait in unemployment lines.
We grow up on the streets.
We live with disabilities.
We are injured in accidents.
We are plagued by family problems.
We fight drug and alcohol abuse.
Have you not heard enough, O God?
We sit in police stations.
We watch our loved ones endure pain.
We are falsely accused.
We encounter prejudice and hate.
We are humiliated and abused.
We contend with unbearable stress and anxiety.
We weep by the grave.

We are your people, O Creator God!
We are the work of your hands.
Is there no more grace
for your troubled ones?
Will we continue
our unholy procession
around the pit
of living death?

There is no sun, no moon, no star.
We cannot see our way.
Have pity on your world, O God,
have pity on your weeping world!

We remember all the times
you lavished your grace
upon our heads
and into our hearts.
You gave us the gift of light,
and we walked with our heads up
in the procession of life.
Restore us, O God,
to your sanctuary.
Look upon us
and let your heart be moved
to break the bonds of the bereaved.
In this hope is our joy.
In that day we will run
to join the procession of life
and we will sing hymns of praise
forever and ever
and ever
and ever!

Lament Psalm Thirty-two

O God, explain to me
the cruelty of your world!
Make sense of those
who make no sense!
Tell me why the innocent die,
and evil people live
to kill again!
Tell me why the faithful
are shunned,
and the self-righteous
point their fingers!
Tell me why the wounded
are wounded,
and sorrow falls
on the shoulder of sorrow!
Tell me why the abused
are abused,
and the victims
victimized!
Tell me why the rains
come to the drowning,
and aftershocks
follow earthquakes.
O God, is this any way
to run a world?
O Merciful One, let us rest
between tragedies!
Speak to us
for we are your people.
Speak to us of hope
for the hopeless

and love for the unloved
and homes for the homeless
and dignity for the dying
and respect for the disdained.

Speak to us, O God,
of the Resurrected One!
Speak to us of hope,
for in spite of
the tidal wave of tears,
we remember your story
of new life!

Tell the world again,
O God of creation!
Tell us that winter will fade,
and spring will wash us new,
and the world will green again,
and we will be new creations
in the garden of our God.
Free us from these tentacles
of sorrow,
and we will fall on our faces
and worship you,
O God of goodness,
O God of a new green world!

Lament Psalm Thirty-three

O God, I'm afraid
to answer my phone
for fear it will be
bad news again.
I live in constant anxiety.
The stress has made me sick!
O God, do you have
a sedative
for my soul?

Has my life with you
been all in vain?
Has my heart been so unworthy?
Has my faithfulness meant nothing?
Long ago
I gave my heart to you,
but it has fallen out.
It lies on the sidewalk
where it's trampled and crushed.
Why have you sent these plagues?
I thought you saved them
for your enemies!
Why can't I walk with you
in peace once more?
Wherever whenever
I have failed you,
I beg your forgiveness.
Wherever I've strayed,
point me back to you!
Whenever I deny you,
call me back.

I kneel in your presence
to say I'm sorry.
Forgive me
and give my life back,
O God!
Forgive me and give
my life back.
Take me from this turmoil.
Give me assurance
of your forgiveness,
for only in you
does life flow.
Only you can stop the tempest
and calm my soul.

You and you only,
only you are holy.
Away from you
my soul has no hope,
but you have promised
to be with your people;
it is in that promise
that I bathe
both day and night.

I hold my soul
in front of your face,
O God!
Take it
in your powerful hands!
Then all my anxiety
will evaporate.

I will know
my soul is safe.

Alleluias spin in my heart!
Thanks be to you,
O Holy One!

Lament Psalm Thirty-four

Tell me, Holy God,
why I have to live
in this unholy hell
on earth?
If all life is holy,
what is this?
And why was I chosen?
Is there some plan
of escape?
Is there some reason
for my captivity?
Do I have to stay here
for the rest of my days?

Look down into hell,
O God,
and see your servant!
Have you confused me
with someone else?
Have you found me guilty
of unfaithfulness?
Have you tried
and convicted me?
Is there no one
to represent me?
Do I have to be
my own counsel?
Am I to burn
in the flames of hell
without a trial?

Pour the water of mercy
on me,
O God of all that is holy!
Pour the water of mercy
on me
again and again!
Free me
from this hole of hell!
Take the tongues of fire
and rest them on my head,
and bless me
with your spirit!
Pull me out
of this living hell,
and I will take
my shoes off,
for you walk on holy ground.
You will make
the whole earth
ablaze
with your holiness!
I will call your name
and hear it echo
throughout the universe
over and over
into eternity!
All will be covered
in holiness.
All will be covered
in holiness.

Lament Psalm Thirty-five

The sky has fallen
and no one seems to notice.
Mountains have fallen
into the sea
and people are oblivious.
Floods cover the land,
and tornadoes topple
the buildings,
and earthquakes
divide the land.
Everywhere I look
there is nothing
but devastation,
and yet,
everyone goes about
their business as usual.
O God, my life
is destroyed,
but people go to the bank
and to the store.
They eat and they drink,
and I crumple
under the weight of my heart.
O God, it is the end
of my world!
Why aren't people
weeping and wailing?
Why isn't the world
on its knees
asking forgiveness?

The whole world is
one great wailing wall
and I will live here
forever!

God Almighty,
why am I all alone?
Couldn't you, O God,
come and sit with me
by the waters of Babylon?
Couldn't you come and
sit with me
on the rubble of the Temple?
Please, O God,
rebuild my world!
Have mercy on me,
for I am all alone.
No one sees that
the sky has fallen,
no one, O God,
no one, but you.
All-knowing God,
you are the only one
who can put the stars
back in place.
Take pity on me
and hold up the sky.

I will walk
by the river of hope,
and you will find me there,
and you will
reach out your hand

and push the heavens back
into place,
and I will kneel
and give thanks,
for you will be with me.
You will put the stars
back in the sky.

Lament Psalm Thirty-six

O God, help me get home!
I am lost
in the forest of fear.
I have no map
except the memory
of your word.
Captive to my fear,
I am frozen
in my anguish,
afraid to move
in any direction.
Which way, O God?
Which way?
Which way leads back home?

O God, find me!
Do not sleep
until I am safely back
by your fireside,
for I shake night and day
with no defense
against the cold,
pelting pain.
I have no sanctuary
against the whipping winds
of fright.
I tremble unshielded
from the hail of suffering.
The trees of terror
grab at me
from every side.

Find me, O caring God,
before night falls,
because I have no light.
Take up your lantern
and look for me
before I die of fright.

I will nestle in the hope
of your coming.
You will find me
and carry me
to the path
that leads home.
I will no longer fear,
for you, O God,
you are my home!

Lament Psalm Thirty-seven

Open your window, O God,
and see me.
Like a wounded bird
lying on the sidewalk,
I wait to be found;
I wait to be helped.

I am too weak
to lift my head.
I open my mouth
to call to you
and nothing comes out.
Even my bones
are fragile.
If you don't
find me soon,
the vultures will
begin to circle.
You, and only you, O God,
can save me.

There have been times
in the past
when I prayed
for your help.
You saw me struggle,
and you gave me your hand.
You have always been there.
Now, O God, I cannot move
on my own.

I can do nothing for myself.
I am completely empty.
If you don't find me,
I will never again
take wing.

I long to hear you stir
and answer my prayer!
Open your window, O God!
Lean out and pick me up
and bring me in!
In your house
I will heal.
With your tender care
I will recover.

I will fly again.
I will fly
through your skies,
and I will sing again.
The words of my song
will be for my God,
my God who watches
for wounded birds.

Lament Psalm Thirty-eight

One day you were here, O God,
and then you disappeared
like a magician
doing tricks
on a stage.

One day we were talking,
and suddenly you turned
silent.
And I spoke only
to the wind.
Have you gone so far away
my voice can no longer
reach you?

Surely you're not
rejecting me
when I am so desolated!
Surely you remember
that I've always
belonged to you!

When I was a child
I flew into your arms
and settled there.
I had no secrets from you.
Now like a baby
abandoned
on a doorstep,
I have awakened
in a strange place
where you do not live.

This is a godless land,
and I do not want
to be here.

Please reappear, O God,
and listen for my prayers!
When you hear me,
your compassion
will fly on the wind;
you will remember
your own
and I will leave
the horror
that I've lived in,
and my feet will walk
next to yours
once more!

Lament Psalm Thirty-nine

What do you want of me,
God who will not leave me alone?
My being is vomited up
on the sidewalk of the city;
I am an emptied shell,
beached and drained of life.
I lie still,
no longer even able
to writhe in pain.
I'm around the corner
from death,
and yet you, O God,
tell me to get up!
You've entered me
in the race again,
and they're already
announcing my name.
Over and over
the loudspeaker blares.
My head is splitting
from the noise.
Don't you know
what bad shape I'm in?
Don't you know
I am weak and unable?
Don't you even remember
what I've been through?

I am the one
who has called your name
over and over,
but I had no loudspeaker.
You did not hear
my crying.
Day after day
and night after night,
I called to you,
but you didn't answer.
You slept
while I wept.
You could have saved me
then, but now I am
completely helpless.
And this is the time
you've chosen
to tell me
to get up and walk!
I can't get up!
I can't even move!
It is too late
to race again.

Withdraw my name!
Take me out of the race!
Stop the loudspeaker;
leave me alone!
Only a miracle
could help me now!

O God of wonder,
you walk the heavens

and light the sun
in the early morning hours.
With compassion
you tend our garden
and our hearts.
When all hope is buried,
you work a miracle:
You plant your strength
in our weakness;
you water our souls,
and we grow to the sun.
And we run in the race.
O God of grace,
thank you!

Lament Psalm Forty

O God, who are these
that gather somewhere
on the lawn of my life
and throw rocks at me?
Haven't I had enough?
Tragedy spits at me
right and left,
but it does not deter
those with
hearts of stone.
They jab at me
and make faces
and judgments
with no attempt
at understanding.

O God, I live
in a tornado
of misery,
yet they pick at me
like chickens
at their grain.
Their mouths are full
of small details,
and their eyes
are closed
to everything
but the images
in their mirrors,
while their ears
shut out my sobbing.

They dress in the letter
of the law,
but the spirit
of the law
is sealed
like unopened mail.

O God, they blaspheme
your word!
Close their mouths,
and melt their hearts,
I pray!

If you will bend near,
I will climb
upon the wings
of your spirit
and soar
from the pit
of despair.
I will write
your word of love
across my face
so that everyone
can see
that I worship you,
the God of forgiveness
and understanding.
Bend near, O God,
for I believe
in the spirit
of your law.

O blessed God,
there is no end
to your mercy.
You smile upon
your hurting children
and turn stone hearts
warm with your love.
Blessed be your name
through all the earth.
Blessed be the spirit
of your compassionate word.

Lament Psalm Forty-one

O God, can't you do anything
for your wounded ones
who walk the earth
in mournful resignation?
We are the ones
who carry our burdens
in silence.
We wear the masks
of everyday politeness,
trying bravely to
hold back the tears
that so readily come.
We walk in loneliness,
not wanting to mar
the joyful lives
of the others.
We are the ones
who cry in the night,
the ones whose hearts pound,
whose stomachs knot,
whose heads split in pain.
We are the ones
who are paralyzed
by fear or shame.
We are the ones
who walk around
with our lives
in upheaval,
hoping against hope
that the worst
will not come.

We are the ones
who kneel before you
now
to pray for your mercy.

Can't you do anything
for us?
Couldn't you at least
take care
of a few of us?
We would be grateful,
for we have compassion
for one another.

You are our God;
we learned mercy
from you.
Wrap your arms
about your wounded ones,
O God, our God,
keep us from harm
for we walk
each day
in the hope of your healing
mercy.

Lament Psalm Forty-two

O God, I am struggling
to survive,
preoccupied with dismal
thoughts
that will not
let me go.
My blood pressure climbs,
and I have aches
and pains
that have no cause except
my broken heart.

Why have you turned
your back on me,
O God?
Why won't you protect me
against my emotions?

I have nowhere to turn
if not to
you.
I have nowhere to go
if not to your
house.
I have no one to talk to
if you won't
talk.
Break your silence
and speak
to me.

Open your door
so I can
get in.
Turn your face to me
and pay attention
to my problems!

Trouble surrounds me
like a fence
with no
gate.
I need eyes in the back
of my head
so I can see
what's coming next.
I'm worn down from trying
to deal
with one hell after another.
The pain in my mind
leaves no room
for rest.
O God, return me
to a life of
joy!
Give me a reason
for
laughter!

Can eyes weep
all
the time?
Can hearts race
night
and day?

Can minds agitate
constantly?
Can my soul survive
this assault?
O God, please
stop this revolving door
of emotional oppression!
Stop the outpouring
of unrelenting
adversity!

O God, on the wings of dawn
you come to my house,
bringing peace
in the palm of your hand.
You open my eyes;
you stand in
my doorway
and invite me
to your house.
O God,
you are my peace!

Lament Psalm Forty-three

We are lost, O Shepherd!
Won't you look
for us?
Your lambs, O God,
have wandered
from your tent.
The wind and rain
beat upon us,
and we were filled with
apprehension
and confused by the
onslaught
of hail.
We panicked and ran
into the night,
where we wander
in circles,
out of range
of your voice
and the warmth
of your fire.
But won't you look
for us?
Our bleating is faint
in the midst
of the storm,
for we've fallen
and we're caught
in the underbrush.

We're here, O Shepherd,
far away from the rest
of the flock,
but won't you look
for us?

Look for us,
O Good Shepherd!
Don't leave a stone
unturned,
for we are shivering
in the night.
We'll never last
until morning!
Dear Shepherd, won't you
look for us?
You are the Good Shepherd!
You will not tolerate
the loss of one lamb!
You will find us
in the night!

Lament Psalm Forty-four

Come to my defense, O God.
They're trying to tell me
how to grieve.
Tell them to leave me
alone.
I don't want to see anybody.
I just want to sit in
my rocking chair
and rock.
I don't want to explain.
I don't want to talk.
I want to be left
alone!

Your people, O God,
are trying
to comfort me;
tell them there is
no comfort.
They're trying
to cheer me;
tell them there is
nothing
that can make me feel
better.
Tell them my name
is Rachel.
Tell them to leave me
alone.

Tell them there's
nothing
on earth
that can help.

And when they're gone,
O God,
come to me!
For without you,
I will wither
and die.
For now
all I can do is
rock
and
wait.
Don't leave me
alone,
O holy God;
don't leave me
alone.

You, O my God,
are my hope.
You are my inheritance,
the gift
of my life.
You have always
poured grace
upon my head.
I wait for you;
I know
you will come
and stand
in my tears.

Lament Psalm Forty-five

O God, hear me!
I'm at the end
of my rope!
I'm at the edge
of the cliff!
I'm in the eye
of the storm!
I'm going down
for the third
time!

O God, are you
going to let me
die?

My dreams, O God,
are gone.
Dead
buried
one after another
gone forever . . .
Am I to be buried
with them?
When dreams die
does the
dreamer
die
with them?

God, O God, O God,
strain your ears
to my prayer.
Search for me
among the
perishing
and pluck me
from the
fire.

O faithful God,
you hear
our prayers
and grab
us
from the jaws
of death.
There is nothing
that can
separate us
from
our God.

Lament Psalm Forty-six

O God, I have eaten of the bread of suffering
and had my fill.
Why have you given me more than my portion?
Sorrow hangs in my heart
like the moon
in the sky,
and
despair covers my shoulders
like a shawl.
Will I grow old
with dread
as my constant companion?

Enough! O God!
Enough!
Stop the plagues
and
let me go!
Push this plate away
from me!
No more!
Never anymore!
Instead let me sit in
the shade of your
kindheartedness
and sip the cool nectar
of blessedness
at your feet.
Raise your hand, O God,
and it will
all be so!

Lift your voice
and night
will turn to day,
and I will rest
in the peace
of your
holy word.

Lament Psalm Forty-seven

I stand at your empty table,
O Holy One,
and ask to be fed.
But there is no bread,
no wine,
no priest.
Is there no one to
minister
to me?
Is there no place
at the table
for
damaged hearts
and
scarred souls?
Do you not invite
everyone who believes?
I believe.
O God,
I believe.
In spite of an empty table,
I believe.
In spite of those who laugh
at me as I wait
for you,
I believe.
In spite of evidence
to the contrary
that they scream
in my face,

I will stand at your empty table,
and wait
until you come,
your arms full of bread,
the wine splashing
as you walk.
Come, O Holy One,
and feed me.

Lament Psalm Forty-eight

I am depressed, O God.
I see no end
to this cycle of sadness.
People tell me:
"Everything will be all right,"
but it isn't,
and it won't be.
They quote Paul to me:
"All things work together for good
for those who love God."
Don't I love you?
Wasn't I brought up
in your holy house,
O God?
Didn't I memorize
your words
and sing hymns to you?
Don't I bow down
to you?
Isn't that what
I'm doing
now?

No one can tell me
any good can come
from this torment!
Let them have their say
if it makes
them feel better!
But I don't want
to hear it!

I know what I've
been through.
I know what it is
to have death
walk the halls
of my home.
What has happened
can't be undone.
What is done cannot
be prettied up.
But you, O God,
can stop
the aftershocks.

O God, tear through
the night
to rescue the one
you have left
too long.
Help me, O Holy God,
out of this tomb
of pain.
Break the cycle
and allow me
to live in your
halcyon holiness.

Only you, O God,
are righteous.
In your righteousness
I will find
a holy place.
My cup runneth over!

Lament Psalm Forty-nine

O God, I wasn't there for him!
Why didn't you let me be there
for him?
When he walked through
the valley of the shadow of death,
I wasn't there to hold him
against the night of fear
or to comfort him
in the atrocity of his pain.
O God, you could have given me that!
You could have allowed me
to be with him
in his hour.

When you called my name,
didn't I come?
And didn't I stay?
Haven't I spent my life
searching for your truth?
O God, where was our covenant
that night?
Where, O God, were you?
What's the sense of all this,
O Mystery?
What's the sense
of all my pain?
What good comes from
my tears?
What is better because
he died?

What is better because
I cried?
The world still spits in
the eye of God.

This is my prayer, O Holy One:
Give me the peace
that passes
understanding.
Give me the assurance
that you were
there for him.
Give me the assurance
that you are here
for me.

O God, in your mysterious power
you make the oceans roar
and the starfish
wash upon the shore.
And my son lives
in the heart of heaven,
and I live
in the heart of earth,
but we live together
in the heart of God.

Lament Psalm Fifty

O God, I walk on coals!
My feet burn
and blister,
but you do not come
to my fiery furnace.

I wander in the desert!
My eyes fill with sand;
they water and sting,
but you do not come
to touch my eyes
to sight again.

I pray to a silent God;
I bow to an absent deity.
What use are my psalms
if you are not here
to listen?
I lament in your sanctuary
and yearn to feel
your tears
mingle with mine,
but it's only my tears
that roll hot
down my face.
O God,
do you walk the halls
of heaven
instead of the alleys
of earth?

I do not ask, O God,
that you scrub away my pain.
I do not ask
that you blot from my mind
the searing scorching memory.
I do ask
that you stand with me
on these coals.
I do ask
that you not let me
wander in the desert alone.

O loving God,
you are the morning star
that breaks the sky
into light.
You are my
alleluia!